When the Music Stopped

The Testament of Nova

Abhinav Agarwal

BookLeaf
Publishing

India | USA | UK

Dedication

For the three hundred and sixty-four young souls

who danced their last dance at dawn—

may your memory be a blessing

and your stories fade into silence.

For those who survived to bear witness—

may you find healing in the telling,

strength in the remembering,

and peace in knowing that your testimony

will resound through generations.

For the families who lost their precious ones—

may you find comfort in community,

solace in memory,

and hope in the knowledge that

your loved ones' light continues to shine.

For the desert that holds these stories—

may you bloom again with life,

may you hear music instead of screams,

may you become both memorial and garden.

Acknowledgement

First and foremost, to the survivors who shared their stories—your courage in bearing witness made this work possible. To the families who opened their hearts and shared memories of their loved ones—your generosity in grief has ensured these stories will never be forgotten.

Special gratitude to:

The Nova Foundation for their healing programs and 24/7 crisis support.

The October 7 Documentation Project for preserving testimonies.

The healing communities that emerged to support survivors and families.

The artists, musicians, and writers

who help transform trauma into
testimony.

The Nova Legal Aid Network
providing pro bono services.
The Memorial Forest Project planting
trees for each victim.

The Digital Memorial Wall preserving
stories and photographs.

The Healing Place offering art therapy
and community programs.

For those seeking support:

The Nova Foundation coordinates trauma
counseling services and maintains a 24/7 crisis
hotline. The Healing Place welcomes
survivors and families for art therapy and
community healing programs. Legal assistance
is available through the Nova Legal Aid
Network.

These poems would not exist without the generous sharing of stories by survivors and families, the meticulous work of documentarians and journalists, and the dedication of healing communities that continue to support recovery and remembrance.

May this work honor your trust and contribute to the enduring labor of memory and healing.

Foreword

Dear Abhinav,

I want to thank you for your courage to dive deep into the open wound that is the October 7th massacre, especially into the horrors that unfolded at the Nova music festival.

As a survivor who was there that morning. who fled for hours with friends through fields and fear. I want to thank you for your choice to investigate, to learn, to listen, and to write. But more than that, I thank you for writing a book that will remain as testimony for generations to come.

For the past year, I've been telling my story. Telling it is, in some ways, the simple part for me - we, the survivors, carry the images in our minds like an always-open photo album. But helping someone feel what happened? That is something else entirely. And you, Abhinav, somehow managed to reach that place, to bring it down from the mind into the body.
Thank you for your courage. Thank you for your heart. Thank you for a book that touches on what we often can't even explain ourselves.

You weren't there. But through your words, you reached into the beating heart of what happened. That's not something to take lightly. It's an act of grace. Of deep listening. Of writing as a sacred calling.

The texts you wrote, the poems, the testimonies, even the simple black-and-white illustrations - manage to reach places words alone often can't. They take us back there. But more than that, they offer others who weren't there a vivid and piercing glimpse of what it was. Chaos, fear, love, escape, the raw choice to live. Sometimes it feels like the experience is beyond description, because our bodies remember more than our words. And somehow, your book goes straight through the mind and into the body. It lets those who weren't there feel. And for those of us who were - it reminds.

For me personally, at first, it broke me, but then it helped rebuild me. It brought me back to my commitment - to live a life of optimism, kindness, and grace. out of deep respect for the life that was almost taken from me. from us.

This book goes beyond documentation. It doesn't just tell, it touches.

It doesn't just report it remembers. And most of all, it leaves us with a question that echoes forward: How do we go on? How do we dance again?

And just as you, Abhinav, found the words to illuminate the darkness, we, the survivors, will continue to seek the light. We will keep telling, sharing, and healing - each of us in our own way.

What echoed in me most throughout your book was the reminder of how vast and varied that day was. October 7th didn't have one face - it had thousands. Each moment, each person, each choice - that day held more stories than can ever be told. But somehow, you honored that.

At Nova, there were 4,400 people. Each one a whole universe. Each one forced to flee for their life.

Three hundred sixty-four souls will never come home again. Will never reunite with family. Will never dance again.

And there are infinite faces - for one single day in October.

Thank you for writing. Thank you for seeing. Thank you for letting it echo - not to drown in the pain, but to live, to connect, to remember, and to cherish.

The desert will hear music again instead of screams. We will dance again.

In memory of the 364 lives taken in a moment, For the survivors - those wounded in body and those carrying the scars in their soul, And for the hostages, for whom October 7th is still happening every day - For them, and for us - we will go on living with light, optimism, and with love.

With deep love and heartfelt gratitude,

Shalev

Preface

This collection was born from a visit to the Nova exhibition in Los Angeles, where the raw power of testimony and memory first took root. Standing among the artifacts, photographs, and stories of that October morning, it became clear that poetry might offer another way to bear witness—not to explain or analyze, but to honor and remember.

This collection contains 107 poems, each drawing from the testimonies of survivors, the grief of families, and the enduring spirit of a community that refuses to let darkness have the final word.

The book is structured in four parts:

Part One: The Morning captures the attack itself, from the peaceful pre-dawn dancing to the horror that followed.

Part Two: The Families explores the devastating impact on those who lost loved ones.
Part Three: The Light honors both heroes and victims, celebrating courage while acknowledging loss.
Part Four: The Healing traces the ongoing journey toward recovery and remembrance.

Each section opens with testimonies from survivors and families, drawn from interviews, news reports, and direct accounts. These carefully curated voices ground our poems in lived experience, ensuring that imagination serves truth rather than overshadowing it.

Through various poetic forms—from free verse to strict sonnets, from haikus to ghazals—these poems attempt to capture both the unspeakable horror of what happened and the indomitable human spirit that survives. Each form serves its purpose: formal structures contain overwhelming grief, while free verse allows for raw emotional expression. Some poems use experimental forms like haibun or double haiku sequences to bridge tradition and trauma.

The collection traces events from dawn on October 7, 2023, through the desperate days of searching, to the final count of 364 victims. It follows the months of captivity, celebrates moments of hope like Noa Argamani's rescue after 246 days, and witnesses triumph rising from tragedy, as when survivor Yuval Raphael won Rising Star in January 2025.

The collection ends with seven poems in Section XXI, bringing our total to 107—a number that mirrors the days of captivity but also points toward future hope. Like the desert itself, these poems hold both memory and possibility, both grief and renewal, both what was lost and what might yet be reclaimed.

This is not just a book of poems—it is a testimony, a memorial, and a promise to remember. Every word here is offered in service of that sacred duty: to ensure that what happened at Nova is never forgotten, never denied, and never repeated.

May these poems serve as candles in the darkness, as witnesses to truth, and as seeds of hope planted in soil that has known too much sorrow.

"Some find God in silence,
some in sacred halls—
we found divinity
in movement,
and lost it
in stillness,
and seek it still
in every beat
that dares us
to dance again."
 - from Section XII: Faith And Dance

Before the World Changed

In the pre-dawn hours of October 7, 2023, the Nova music festival was a celebration of life, music, and spiritual freedom. For 23-year-old Danielle Gelbaum, dancing was liturgy: "Some people pray at church...I pray when I'm on the dance floor...That's where I go to feel free," she would later recall.

Under fading stars on the festival grounds near Kibbutz Re'im, 3,500 souls—ravers, meditators, soldiers on leave—swayed as one. Few noticed the flicker of paragliders on the horizon, or the way dawn's first light bled crimson over Gaza's fence, 5 kilometers away. No one could know that these moments of

pure celebration would be their last taste of
innocence, that the rising sun would soon
usher in unimaginable horror.

These poems capture those final hours of
peace, when the music still held magic and
the dawn promised only another beautiful
day.

Last Dance

The bass thrumming deep beneath our feet,
earth's own heartbeat matching ours
as we lift our arms to stars
that haven't yet begun to fade.

Three thousand souls
pulse as one beneath
the desert's vast embrace,
our bodies writing prayers
in the language of movement,
in the scripture of the present.

This is our temple:
laser lights piercing darkness,
bare feet on sacred ground,
sweat like a baptism
in the cool night air.

We are infinite in this moment,
immortal in this space
between midnight and dawn,
between earth and sky,
between what was
and what will be.

If we had known—
but we didn't know,
couldn't know,
as we danced our last dance
with the night,
that these were the final hours
of who we once used to be.

Desert Stars Fade

Night sky retreats
over Re'im's silence—
music pulses on

Dawn approaches slow
through purple-shadowed air
while we dance below

Stars surrender now
to morning's gentle touch—
one last sacred bow.

Prayer in Motion

The music wraps around us like prayer shawls,
and we move as if possessed by something
holy. Bodies become offerings, sweat turns to
incense in the cool pre-dawn air. We are all
prophets here, all pilgrims, all seekers finding
God in the bass line, in the drum beat, in the
way our feet kiss the earth with each step. The
desert holds us in its ancient palms as we

dance our devotions. Some find their temple
in stone buildings, some in synagogues, some
in mosques—but here, under the fading stars,
we have built our own sanctuary of sound and
movement. We are writing psalms with our
bodies, singing hymns with our motion, these
moments as pure as any prayer ever
whispered within sacred walls. We don't know
yet that this is our last service, our final
communion. We are still innocent, still
anointed, still free.

Dawn's Innocence

The stars grow dim as morning creeps above
the eastern hills; their ancient light gives way
to something tender. We dance our endless
love—
for life itself, while night becomes the day.
Three thousand hearts beat wild beneath the
sky,
our bodies write their stories in the air,
and music lifts our spirits soaring high
we touch the face of God without a care.
If we could freeze this moment, hold it fast—

this perfect peace before the world awakes—
perhaps we'd see the shadow that was cast,
perhaps we'd feel the ground before it breaks.
But innocence knows nothing of its end;
we dance on still, too blessed to comprehend.

What We Could Not Know

Desert wind carries
murmurs of rusted wire uncoiling—
we laugh, spin, ignite.

Morning approaches, armed with truths
our bliss could never decrypt.

Safe in our beautiful blindness,
we chart constellations
in the glow of phones
that will soon flood with final pleas:
"I love you. Tell them. Tell the world."

When The Sky Fell

The transition from celebration to terror arrived with the first blush of dawn. As Millet Ben Haim recalled, "It was just a massive barrage, tons of rockets flying above our head." For the thousands of festival-goers, the initial moments brought confusion—rocket fire was no stranger to the region. But this was different. Rada Rashed, working as a caterer that morning, witnessed the celebration transform into chaos and carnage as militants opened fire on the crowd. These poems capture that shattering instant when the world tilted on its axis, when music gave

way to sirens, and dawn's promise curdled
into a nightmare.

The First Alarm

The sirens fracture our electric dreams,
as rockets rip through morning sky apart.
Nothing here is quite the way it seems.

The music stops. A thousand voices scream
as terror clutched each unsuspecting heart.
The sirens fracture our electric dreams.

Red tracers paint their deadly laser beams
across the dawn—this is no warning dart.
Nothing here is quite the way it seems.

Our sanctuary, now a trap that teems
with danger as the real nightmares start.
The sirens shatter our electric dreams.

The desert air fills up with desperate themes
of flight and fear—we're falling all apart.
Nothing here is quite the way it seems.

This can't be real, our minds refuse these scenes
of paradise transformed to horror's art.
The sirens shatter our electric dreams.
Nothing here is quite the way it seems.

Last Call

My phone buzzes against my racing heart
as father's name lights up the screen.
Like Shahar, I answer—
what else can I do
in this moment suspended between
what was and what will be?

"I love you," I say,
because these might be
the last words he'll ever hear
from my lips.

He knows by my voice
that I'm saying goodbye,
knows from the gunfire
crackling through the connection
that his child stands

on the edge of existence.

The call drops.
The world drops.
Everything we knew
drops away.

Red Dawn

Rockets split the morning sky, a deadly rain
Echoing across the desert plain where we
Believed ourselves untouchable. Now pain
Obliterates that dream. We try to flee,
Rushing nowhere, everywhere, as rounds
Nip at our heels and terror pounds.

Warning Signs

Dawn breaks, blood-red now—
rockets tear through morning peace—
music dies mid-beat

Screams replace the bass—
festival becomes fury—
paradise turns hell

Bullets slice the air—
where dancers raised their arms high,
bodies collapse low.

First Blood

Bullets crack
through morning silence
like glass

Terror sweeps
across the dancing ground
like fire

We scatter
like startled birds but
some fall

Dreams shatter
in the rising sun's
red glare.

No Way Out

As the reality of the attack became clear, panic erupted across the festival grounds. Danielle Gelbaum witnessed the unthinkable: "Every few minutes, hearing a gunshot and seeing a kid falling down in front of my eyes." The festival grounds became a maze of death, with every escape route seemingly blocked. Noa Argamani and others found their cars useless: "We drove toward the exit and suddenly they started shooting at us. We turned and everywhere we went we were shot at." Some, like Rada Rashed, found temporary sanctuary in holes or ditches: "Bullets were hitting near my face... The girls around were shot down, and I was waiting to get hit. Then I saw a hole... We went into it." These poems capture the desperate search for safety when there was nowhere safe left to run.

Running in Circles

We run, but there is nowhere left to run,
each path leads back to terror's open jaw.
The morning sun becomes a burning gun,
our paradise transformed to nature's raw.

Each path leads back to terror's open jaw,
cars crammed like cattle in a slaughter pen.
Our paradise transformed to nature's raw—
we're prey now, we who danced as free
women.

Cars jammed like cattle in a killing pen,
bullets etch their names across the sky.
We're prey now, we who danced as free
women,
watching friends drop, not knowing why.

Bullets write their names across the sky,
the morning sun becomes a burning gun.
Watching friends drop, not knowing why,
we run, but there is nowhere left to run.

The Pit

Like Rada, we found salvation
in the earth's dark mouth—
a pre-dug hole, maybe
for construction, maybe
for graves. Who's to stay?
Who cares? It holds us now.

Six of us pressed together,
breathing dust and terror,
while above our heads
bullets snap like angry wasps,
seeking flesh to sting.

A girl falls near the edge,
her blood drips down
like dark rain.
We dare not pull her in—
movement means death,

and we are choosing life
second by second,
breath by breath,
in this pit that is both
sanctuary and tomb.

Gridlock

Metal coffins lined up on the road,
engines running, going nowhere fast.
Every window holds a different load
of terror as the die is finally cast.
We're rabbits in the hunter's deadly game,
all our choices ending just the same.

The car ahead erupts in sudden flame,
behind us screams announce another hit.
No time to speak each victim's sacred name,
as bullets find their marks and bodies split.
We abandon what we thought was safe—
our wheels, our hopes, our faith.

The Fallen

They fall like petals in a sudden storm,
these dancers who just touched the morning
sky.
No time for grace, no chance to say goodbye,
as bullets find them, still so young, so warm.

A boy drops mid-stride, phone still in his
hand,
perhaps his mother on the other end
will hear his final breath, will comprehend
what we ourselves can barely understand.

A girl in glitter shorts becomes a star
falling to earth—her sparkles catch the sun
as she collapses, dreams left half-undone,
her future scattered near her fallen car.

We count the bodies as we run past each,
knowing we could join them at a breath.
This field becomes an altar unto death,
with sacrifice beyond our power to reach.

The Choice

Some paths lead to bullets,
some to barbed wire—
choose quickly now.

Left or right? The choice
might mean life or death.
No time to think.

Like Noa in the woods,
we hide, we run, we pray—
but prayers don't stop lead.

Some will live because
they turned this way, not that.
Some will die the same.

Fate plays roulette with
footsteps in the sand—
each choice our last, perhaps.

Places of Shadow

In the desperate search for safety, survivors found refuge in whatever shelter they could find. Millet Ben Haim and three other women crouched behind a single bush for six harrowing hours, hearing Hamas fighters "laughing as they shot people." Yuval Raphael endured eight unbearable hours in a concrete bomb shelter, ultimately surviving by hiding beneath the bodies of those who didn't. Michal Ohana spent nine terrifying hours motionless under a tank, playing dead. These poems capture the agonizing hours spent in these makeshift sanctuaries, where the line between shelter and trap often blurred, where silence meant survival, and where every breath might be the last.

Under Metal

Beneath the car's hot belly,
I press my cheek to the earth,
tasting dust and motor oil,
feeling the engine's dying warmth
against my back.

Boots pass inches from my face—
I count the steps, hold my breath,
pray to become invisible,
smaller than small,
nothing at all.

A shell casing drops,
clinks against concrete
like a tiny bell
tolling for the dead,
for the dying,
for those of us
caught in between.

Oil drips black tears
onto my shoulder,
marking me as one

of the hidden ones,
the maybe-alive,
the not-yet-dead.

The Bush

Four women pressed against a desert bush,
its branches slender as hope against the sky.
We hardly dare to breathe or blink or sigh
as footsteps circle in the morning's hush.
Their laughter drifts upon the wind, they
crush
the life from those they find—we hear each
cry,
each plea cut short. We understand that I
might be the next whose voice they'll force to
shush.

Six hours pass like centuries of fear.
The bush becomes our mother, holds us close,
while just beyond, death stalks in desert heat.
Their voices fade, return, fade, reappear—
until at last, when evening nearly shows,
salvation comes on rescue workers' feet.

Tank's Shadow

Nine hours frozen still
under steel, playing dead while
killers prowl above—
each breath might be the last one,
each heartbeat a betrayal

Michal counts seconds
that stretch to infinity—
metal shields her now,
but any shift or whisper
could transform shield into tomb.

Fragile Peace

There comes a lull in the sound,
As silence settles around.
But we've learned to know
That quiet's for show—
More terror waits to be found.

The shooting seems far away,
Some think it's safe now to stray.
But those who rise

Meet their demise—
The hunters are still at play.

Living Grave

In the concrete shelter, we press together,
thirty bodies seeking refuge in shadows. The
space meant for twenty now holds more, and
still they come. Someone whispers a prayer.
Someone else sobs. We try to quiet
them—sound is death now.
A grenade rolls in.
Flash. Thunder. Screams.
When consciousness returns, I find myself
buried. Not in earth, but in flesh. Bodies of
friends, of strangers, have fallen on me. Their
weight should crush me, but instead it shields
me. For hours, I lie beneath my dead
companions as the killers return again and
again, shooting into the pile to ensure their
work is complete. I learn to breathe without
moving my chest. I learn to exist between
heartbeats. I learnt that survival sometimes
means becoming one with the dead.

morning light finds us—
eleven still breathing souls
among the fallen

What Eyes Cannot Unsee

Some survivors witnessed horrors that would eternally haunt them. Rada Rashed watched helplessly as "Young women at the festival were begging Hamas members not to kill them... But they were having fun with them. They took them by their hair and shot them in the head." Noa Argamani's terrified face became one of the massacre's most haunting images as she was torn from her boyfriend and carried away on a militant's motorcycle. Millet Ben Haim, hiding behind a bush, heard the attackers "laughing as they shot people...

They were confident. I knew they would have
no mercy." These poems capture the moments
when survivors came face to face with pure
evil, witnessing atrocities that would sear
themselves into memory forever.

Mercy's End

They beg for life beneath the rising sun,
young women kneeling in the blood-soaked
sand.
The killers laugh—their sport has just begun.

Their prayers are silenced by the brutal gun,
their hair clenched tight in some uncaring
hand.
They beg for life beneath the rising sun.

Each execution is a story spun
in horror—death we can't yet understand.
The killers laugh—their sport has just begun.

Through Rada's eyes, we see them, one by one,
fall silent as their futures turn to sand.
They beg for life beneath the rising sun.

No mercy here—all innocence undone,
by those who treat death like a game they've
planned.
The killers laugh—their sport has just begun.

When darkness falls, the horror's course is
run,
but memory burns like some infernal brand:
They begged for life beneath the rising sun.
The killers laughed—their sport had just
begun.

The Motorcycle

In that moment caught on film,
Noa reaches back toward Avinatan,
her face a mask of terror
we now wear in recurring nightmares.

The motorcycle roars,
carrying her into darkness
while her love stands frozen,
hand still stretched toward
where she used to be.

This is how worlds end:
not with a bang
but with a girl's scream
dissolving into distance,
with a boy's desperate reach
grasping only air,
with a future
snapped like a thread
between two hearts.

Laughter in Hell

They laugh while killing—this we can't
unhear:
the sound of joy in murder's evil face.
Young bodies fall like toys that children steer
and knock down, leaving death in beauty's
place.

The sound of joy in murder's evil face
rings louder than the gunshots or the screams.
And knock down, leaving death in beauty's
place,

they treat our terror like their pleasant
dreams.

Rings louder than the gunshots or the
screams,
their mirth, their casual sport of ending life.
They treat our terror like their pleasant
dreams,
while friends fall silent beneath their knife.

Their mirth, their casual sport of ending
life—
young bodies fall like toys that children steer.
While friends fall silent beneath their knife,
they laugh while killing—this we can't unhear.

What Rada Saw

He saw them beg, these daughters of the
dawn,
their hands raised up in prayer or
supplication,
each plea cut short, each mercy swiftly gone,
each death a separate annihilation.

They took such pleasure in their power then,
these men who played with life like careless
gods,
who pulled girls up by hair, then watched
them when
they fell, their bodies crumpling into clods.

No reason given, no explanation made—
just laughter echoing across the sand,
as one by one, these angels were unmade,
their futures scattered by some monstrous
hand.

Remember them: their terror and their grace,
their final moments in this cursed place.

The Witness

What eyes have seen, the heart must bear
through all the nights that lie ahead.
No dawn can cleanse this care.
What eyes have seen, the heart must bear—
each memory a silent prayer
for peace to find the tortured dead.

What eyes have seen, the heart must bear
through all the nights that lie ahead.

Torn Apart

In the chaos of the attack, families and loved ones were brutally separated. Danielle Gelbaum's singular focus became saving her sister Lior, vowing "There's no way I was going back home, facing my parents and saying: 'Hi mom and dad, I survived but your other kid... she was murdered.'" Jenny Sividia went to the festival not knowing her brother Shlomi was there too—only one would survive. Noa Argamani's last glimpse of her boyfriend Avinatan was as she was carried away on a motorcycle, reaching back toward him in desperate terror. These poems capture the agony of separation, the desperate phone

calls, and the haunting uncertainty of not
knowing who lived and who died.

Two Sisters

DANIELLE:
Run, Lior, run—
don't look back,
don't stop,
don't let go
of my hand.

LIOR:
The bullets—
they're so close—
I can't—

DANIELLE:
You can.
You must.
I won't go home
without you.
I won't face them
alone.

LIOR:
Others are falling—

DANIELLE:
We're not others.
We're sisters.
We're one heart
split between
two bodies.
Both or neither—
that's the deal
we make with fate.

BOTH:
Run.
Just run.
Together.

Last Message Sent

The phone screen glows with one last chance
to say
goodbye, or maybe not—we still have hope
that silence doesn't mean what we all fear.
The signal bars fade in and out like time

itself has started stuttering. Each call
might be the last thread binding love to life.

"I love you," words so simple, yet their life
depends on reaching through the void to say
what matters most. We make that final call
because it's all we have to give us hope:
a voice, a text, a promise that in time
we'll meet again. We push away our fear.

But in each static pause, we taste the fear
that grows between each breath, each pulse of
life.
The messages send slowly, and the time
between responses stretches. What to say
when words might be your last? We cling to
hope
like drowning swimmers waiting for the call.

Then suddenly—the final, fatal call
drops dead. The silence confirms our fear.
The screen goes dark, and with it dies our
hope
of reaching through the chaos into life.
There's nothing left for anyone to say.

The messages stop marking passing time.

We'll spend the rest of our remaining time
remembering that last unfinished call,
those broken words we didn't get to say,
the static-filled goodbye. We'll feed our fear
with every unanswered ping, while life
goes on without the comfort of our hope.

(Some say we shouldn't cling to so much
hope,
that we should learn to live with loss, in time.
But how do you surrender half your life
when every ring might be that rescued call,
when every shadow holds both love and fear,
when there's so much we still need to say?)

Hope dies with each unanswered call.
Time stretches endless in this realm of fear.
Life stops between the words we couldn't say.

Brother and Sister

Jenny dances joy—
unaware her brother's here

sharing the same sky

Shlomi somewhere near
in the pre-dawn festival—
paths that never cross

Morning brings the storm
siblings scattered in the wind—
one falls, one survives

Blood ties cannot save
what fate has determined must
be forever split

Memory carries
what arms cannot hold—brother
still dancing in dreams.

Noa's Reach

That moment caught in time: her hand
stretched back
toward his, their fingers almost touching
there

like God and Adam on the chapel's air—
but this is Eden's opposite, the lack

of grace, of mercy. On the motorcycle's track
she's carried from his reach, beyond his
prayer,
her terror frozen in a camera's stare,
while he stands helpless on the gunfire's rack.

Two hundred forty-six long days she'll spend
in Gaza's darkness, calling out his name
while he searches every way to find her soul.
Their love story, suspended without end,
burns bright against the backdrop of their
pain:
two hearts still reaching toward their broken
whole.

Signals Lost

The towers are down.
Calls won't go through.
Each "Message Failed"
another small death.

We keep trying—
what else can we do
when half our heart
might still be beating
somewhere out there
in the killing fields?

Press "Send" again.
And again.
And again.
Until the battery dies
or we do.

One bar of signal—
a miracle:
"I love you"
goes through.

No reply comes.
We'll never know
if they read it
before the end.

Beneath The Dead

Some of the most haunting survivor accounts come from those who lived by hiding beneath the bodies of those who died. Yuval Raphael endured eight hours in a concrete bomb shelter, surviving only by hiding under fallen victims as militants returned repeatedly to shoot anyone still alive. "When their bodies... fell on us, I understood that hiding under them was the only way I could survive the nightmare," she recalled. Noa Ben Artzi found herself pinned under multiple corpses after a grenade attack, one body's head pressing against her throat, discovering that her only companion in that tomb of flesh—a woman named Michele whom she had comforted earlier—was also still alive. These poems capture the unimaginable experience of finding life among death, of becoming one with the fallen to survive.

Under Bodies

First comes the grenade's thunder, then darkness, then the weight. You wake to find yourself buried, not in earth but in flesh. The dead become your blanket, your shield, your salvation. Someone's arm lies across your throat—you dare not move it. Someone's chest presses against your cheek—you learn to breathe through the spaces between ribs. The blood that drips is not your own, but it marks you all the same. You know their names, some of them. Just minutes ago, they were people with voices and dreams. Now they are your armor against those who would make you join them. Hours pass like centuries. The killers return, shooting into the pile to ensure their work is complete. You master the art of being corpse-still, of existing between heartbeats. The dead keep their final vigil over you, these

reluctant guardians, these sacred shields. You
survive because they did not, and this debt
will mark you forever.

Yuval's Hours

Eight hours beneath
this weight of flesh,
this shield of souls.
I count the bodies:
three, maybe four
pressed against me,
through me, into me.

They return again,
and again, these hunters
of the almost-dead,
shooting into our pile
to silence any heart
that dares still beat.

I learn to breathe
without breathing,
to live without living,
to become as still
as those who shelter me.

Eleven of us
emerge alive
from this tomb of forty.
The numbers tattoo
themselves behind my eyes:
11 from 40,
living from dead,
spared by the sacrifice
of unwitting angels.

Michele and Noa

Two strangers huddled in the dark before,
now pressed together under layers of dead.
We dare not whisper through the shelter door
while killers prowl with measured, ruthless
tread.

Now bound together under layers of dead,
your heartbeat whispers next to mine—still
here.
While killers prowl with their measured,
ruthless tread,
we share each breath, each pulse of silent fear.

Your heartbeat whispers next to mine—still
here,
though bodies stack like sandbags on our
backs.
We share each breath, each pulse of silent
fear,
as gunshots ring and smoke the shelter cracks.

Though bodies pile like sandbags on our
backs,
we dare not whisper through the shelter door.
As gunshots ring and smoke the shelter
cracks,
two strangers huddled in the dark before.

The Weight

They press against us now, these sacred dead,
their cooling flesh our shield against the
storm,
each body that could break us serves instead
to keep our hidden hearts still beating warm.

We know their names, remember how they
stood
just moments past, alive with dance and song.
Now martyred angels in this brotherhood
of flesh, they help us silently along.

The hours stretch beneath this human shield,
as killers stalk above with careful tread.
We owe our breath to those who had to yield
their lives that we might borrow from the
dead.

How do you thank the ones whose final grace
was just to fall and shield your hiding place?

Resurrection

When rescue finally comes, we must be
excavated like artifacts from an ancient tomb.
Each body lifted away peels a piece of us with
it—we have become one with our protectors,
these unwitting saviors who died so we could
live. The rescuers' hands reach down through
strata of death to find us, pull us up into a
world we're no longer sure we belong to. We
emerge like newborns, blinking in the harsh
light, our skin imprinted with the patterns of
the dead, our lungs remembering how to take
full breaths again. We are archeological finds:
survivors preserved in flesh instead of amber,
stories trapped in bone and blood.

   morning light reveals
   what night has made of us all—
   the saved, the saviors

   we rise from our tomb
   marked forever by those who
   fell that we might live

A Mother's War

The massacre created two kinds of maternal grief: those who lost children, and those whose children survived but were forever changed. Juliana Bausi, who lost her only son Itay, expressed her devastation: "My life is a nightmare. 'Surreal doesn't even come close. Our lives are shattered." Roni Katz, described the heartbreaking task of caring for her traumatized 30-year-old son: "He is 30 years old. I fed him with a spoon... I placed a baby monitor under his mattress. I'm afraid to leave the house." These poems capture both forms of maternal grief—the hollow silence of absence, and the aching endurance of

presence. The void, and the vigil. The ones
who never came back, and the ones who did,
but with ghosts in their eyes.

What Remains

My baby boy lies silent in the sand,
no mother's arms to hold him as he sleeps.
The desert claims what I can't understand:
this child of mine, this treasure I can't keep.

They found him where he fell, trying to save
the others—always thinking of their pain.
My soldier son, my medic, strong and brave,
now just a body in the morning rain.

The funeral rites bring me no relief,
no comfort in the prayers that others say.
There is no balm for this specific grief:
a mother's heart that dies day after day.

I water earth with tears that will not end,
and whisper to a son who can't respond.
No grave can hold the love that I must tend,
no death unbinds this everlasting bond.

Feeding My Son

At thirty, he becomes
an infant again—
I lift the spoon
to trembling lips,
coax each swallow
like decades ago.

He sits on the balcony,
clutching a knife,
muttering "Mom,
so they won't kill you,
so they won't kill you."
I dare not sleep.

The baby monitor
beneath his mattress
carries his nightmares
to my waiting ears—
every whimper,
every terror-filled cry.

My son came home
but someone else lives
in his skin,
wears his face,
speaks with his voice,
haunts his eyes.

I feed him with a spoon
and pray:
let him find his way
back to himself,
back to me,
back to life.

Two Mothers

Each morning I wake to feed my broken
child,
While somewhere you tend only a grave, my
child.

Your son lies still beneath October's sand,
Mine rocks and moans, half-saved, my child.

You kiss cold stone and speak to silent air,
I hold warm flesh that's still half-enslaved, my
child.

Your grief has edges, borders I can't know,
While mine flows endless like a wave, my
child.

Both of us mothers of October's sons—
One lost to death, one to the pain that's
graved, my child.

Night Watch

A mother sits guard in the night,
While her son battles dreams full of fright.
  The monitor beeps,
   As fitfully sleeps
The boy who survived but's not right.

She watches him pace with his blade,
Protecting from ghosts that won't fade.
  "They won't hurt you here,"
   She whispers, though fear
Still stalks through the peace they once made.

The Empty Room

I keep his bed made,
his clothes folded
in drawers that will
never open again.

Dust settles on
his running shoes,
his medical texts,
his half-drunk
water glass.

Sometimes I imagine
I hear his key
in the door,
his voice calling
"Mom, I'm home!"

But only silence
answers now,
and I tend this
museum of memory
like a garden

that will never
bloom again.

Every morning,
I wake up and
remember:
my baby boy
is gone.

Every night,
I go to sleep and
pray this is just
a nightmare.

But morning comes,
and he is still
twenty-two forever,
while I age
without him.

Blood Bonds

The massacre created a particular kind of heartbreak for siblings. Jenny Sividia, 41, went to the festival not knowing her brother Shlomi, 37, was there too—only one would have made it out alive. Ofri Rahum lost multiple family members: "Rahum's sister, who was four months pregnant, her sister's fiancé, and Rahum's uncle were all killed at the Nova party." For Ofri, time stopped that day: "It's as if they went on a trip, and we are waiting for them to come back." These poems explore the unique anguish of sibling loss, the survivor's guilt of those who lived while their

brothers or sisters died, and the unbreakable
bonds that persist long after death.

One Heart Split

We shared one womb, one childhood, and one
home,
now sharing only memories and pain.
I dance in sunlight while you sleep alone
beneath the earth that drinks October's rain.

They tell me time will heal, but how can this
be healed—this amputation of the soul?
Each mirror shows your face I'll always miss,
each laugh reminds me we're no longer whole.

You're four months gone, your baby never
born,
your future stolen on that blood-soaked
ground.
I walk these streets, by grief and memory
torn,
while you lie silent, never to be found.

Time flies, they say, but mine stands frozen
still—
waiting for you, as it forever will.

Waiting Room

Morning light filters
through hospital windows—hope
fades with each report

Sister's empty bed
where machines kept vigil now
holds only silence

Your child unborn sleeps
forever in your stillness—
two hearts stopped as one

Memory carries
what arms cannot hold—your laugh
lingers in my dreams

Time refuses to
move forward without you here—
clock hands frozen still.

The Dance We'll Never Share

The wedding dress hangs like a ghost
in your closed room—the dreams we lost
that morning when the bullets flew.
No sister's dance, no "I do,"
no future that we'd counted cost.

Your fiancé, like you, was tossed
into death's arms. We're doubly crossed
by fate that stole not one but two—
   the wedding dress

now haunts me most.
Your joy in life, the love you'd glossed
across your days—all torn in two.
I live, but half of me died too,
that morning when we paid the cost—
   the wedding dress.

What Jenny Carries

I wear three hats now:
psychologist,

grieving sister,
survivor.

But really, I wear
only your absence,
Shlomi,
draped like a second skin.

We danced that night
under the same stars,
breathed the same air,
never knowing
we shared the space
for the last time.

Now every action
orbits around
having lost you—
my brother,
my mirror,
my what-might-have-been.

The trauma grows
like organic waste,
feeding something new:

this garden of grief
where I cultivate
your memory.

Blood Echo

Some bonds transcend the grave's dark door,
some loves refuse to bow to death.
Though you're not here anymore,
I feel you in my every breath.

Some loves refuse to bow to death,
like shared blood singing in my veins.
I feel you in my every breath,
your presence easing all my pains.

Like shared blood singing in my veins,
your memory flows through every day.
Your presence easing all my pains,
though you have gone so far away.

Your memory flows through every day,
though you're not here anymore.
Though you have gone so far away,
some bonds transcend the grave's dark door.

The Darkest Depths

For some survivors, the trauma proved unbearable. Shirel Golan survived the Nova massacre, only to take her own life one year later, on her 22nd birthday. Her brother, Eyal, shared that she had "received almost no official support" in her struggle with severe post-trauma. Michal Ohana, a veterinary nurse, found she "can't stand the sight of blood" after her ordeal, making it impossible to return to her profession. Roni Katz's son fled to Thailand, suffering such severe PTSD that his mother had to bring him home and care for him as though he were an infant. These poems explore the devastating psychological aftermath of survival, when the war continues long after the bullets stop.

Shirel's Last Birthday

You survived October but October didn't survive in you. For one year you carried it like a second heart, pulsing terror in your chest, like a shadow that grew longer as your own flickered shorter. They say you got out of the car that morning—some premonition saving you while your friends drove on to a different fate. But maybe death just chose to take you slowly, to let October work through your veins like poison, to let you count down three hundred and seventy-eight days until your twenty-second birthday. Your mother took early retirement to watch over you, but who can guard against the darkness when it takes root inside? The Nova Foundation tried to help, but how do you heal a wound that keeps growing? "The State of Israel murdered my sister twice," your brother said. "Once in October, mentally, and a second time today, physically." You chose your birthday to

leave—the day that marked your beginning
became your end. Perhaps because birthdays
remind us we're still here, still breathing, still
carrying what we saw, what we heard, what
we can't forget. You survived October, but
October never stopped killing you.

The Unseen Wound

The mind builds walls
where there were none,
turns ordinary sounds
into gunshots,
ordinary shadows
into predators,
ordinary life
into a minefield
of triggers.

Blood on an animal's paw
becomes blood on sand,
becomes screams in darkness,
becomes bodies falling,
becomes everything
you can't unsee.

The therapist says
"breathe through it"
but breath itself
is suspect now—
each inhale reminds you
of holding it,
of playing dead,
of surviving
when others didn't.

Some nights,
the only way to sleep
is by not sleeping at all.
Some days,
the only way to live
is to pretend
you're someone else,
someone who never
danced at Nova,
someone who still
believes in mornings.

Flight Response

Panic rises fast—
heart pounds against prison ribs,
mind seeks escape routes

Thailand's beaches call—
paradise cannot erase
what memory holds

But terror follows
across oceans,
finds you even there
in paradise,
until mother comes
to bring you home,
to feed you with a spoon,
to guard your dreams
with baby monitors,
to help you relearn
how to be human
all over again.

Night Terrors

The dreams come.
Always the dreams.
Running.
Falling.
Bullets in sand.

Wake screaming.
Check the doors.
Check the windows.
Check the shadows.
Check your pulse.

Knife in hand.
Guard the balcony.
Protect mother.
Protect what's left.
Protect. Protect.

Sleep won't come.
Shouldn't come.
Sleep means dreams.
Dreams mean Nova.
Nova means death.

Dawn breaks.
Nothing breaks.
Everything broken
already.
Still breaking.

State of Abandonment

They left us to our private hells,
each survivor alone,
to battle demons no one sees,
to carry weights unknown.

The state that failed to save us then
fails now to heal our pain.
Some battles end when bullets stop—
this war burns in the brain.

We count our dead in different ways:
some bodies in the ground,
some spirits lost to trauma's maze,
some minds no longer found.

Young Shirel chose her birthday grave
when hope at last ran dry.
Some survived that morning's rage
to choose a slower way to die.

Who counts the cost of healing lost,
of help that never came?
Who marks the graves of those who lived
through Nova, died from shame?

The state denies its second sin:
abandoning the saved.
Some wars end swift with victory,
some smolder to the grave.

Light In Darkness

Amid the horror, heroes emerged. Itay Bausi, a combat medic home on leave, chose to stay and tend to the wounded even as bullets flew. Shani Gabay, though shot in the leg, continued guiding others to safety until her final moments. Mark Shindel shouted a warning that saved others but drew the attackers' attention to himself. An 88-year-old Holocaust survivor opened his home to shelter Daniel Vaknin, the DJ, proving that the light of human compassion can shine even in the darkest moments. These poems honor those who, facing unspeakable evil, chose to help others—some surviving to

tell their tales, others making the ultimate
sacrifice.

The Medic's Choice

When others fled the killing ground that day,
Young Itay chose, against all odds, to stay.
His medic's bag became a sacred shield
As bullets rained across the festival field.
No time to think of safety or of flight
When wounded souls cried out into the night.
His mother's son, in uniform or free,
Could never turn from others' agony.
He worked until the very end drew near,
His healing hands steady despite his fear.
They found him where he fell, still trying to
save
The others—to the last, so young, so brave.
  Some heroes wear their courage like a
crown;
  Some, like Itay, wear it as their shroud.

The Holocaust Survivor's Door

The old man opens his door without
hesitation—eighty-eight years of survival have
taught him what matters. He sees the terror
in the young DJ's eyes and recognizes it: the
same haunted look his generation wore in
darker times. No words needed. He pulls
Daniel inside, away from the gunfire, away
from the hunters. History repeats, but so does
hope. So does courage. So does the human
will to shelter another in the storm.

two generations
of survival meet here—
sanctuary found

old hands shelter youth
passing torch of hope forward
through darkest dawn

Shani's Last Guide

Shot in the leg but still
she wouldn't stop—

pointing the way east
toward Moshav Patish,
away from the killing fields.

Her father racing south
to save her,
while she saved others,
each step a victory
over pain,
each direction given
a final gift.

Four young women
tried to carry her
when she could no longer walk,
but some lights
are destined to fade
so others might find
their way home.

They found her later,
one among many,
but her last act
still guides us:
showing how to live,

how to give,
even as we die.

Mark's Warning

He saw the danger closing in,
The hunters drawing near.
One shout could save the others, win
Them time—but cost him dear.

"Be careful, terrorists!" he cried,
His voice a final flare
That lit the morning as he died,
A beacon of despair.

His warning drew their deadly aim,
Drew bullets to his breast,
But others lived to speak his name,
To tell how they were blessed

By one young man who chose to give
His life that they might flee.
Some heroes die that we might live—
Some lights we'll never see.

To Those Who Drove Into Danger

Here's to the civilians who turned back,
Like Rami Davidyan, who chose to drive
Into the fire when others fled—
Here's to Leon Bar, who saved so many
Before the bullets found him.

Here's to every anonymous hero
Who stopped to pull another into their car,
Who shared their hiding place,
Who held a stranger's hand,
Who whispered comfort in the dark.

Here's to the first responders
Who came too late for some
But just in time for others,
Who carried out the wounded
Under constant fire.

Here's to the old man
Who remembered his own darkness
And opened up his door,
Who proved that even after Auschwitz,
Even after everything,

The light of human kindness
Still outshines the dark.

Here's to every hero,
Named and unnamed,
Who lived to tell their story
Or died to save another—
Your light still guides us
Through this longest night.

Faith And Dance

For many at Nova, the festival was more than just music—it was spiritual communion. Danielle Gelbaum described dancing as her form of prayer: "Some people pray at church; some people pray at the synagogue...I pray when I'm on the dance floor...That's where I go to feel free." After surviving, she found that returning to dance brought both healing and heartbreak: "There is not even one time that I don't have memories of my friends who were murdered... There's no way I'm on the dance floor and not thinking of them." These poems explore the sacred dimension of movement, the festival as a form of

communion, and how survivors struggle to
reconcile faith and joy after witnessing such
horror.

Dancing Queen

Before the bullets came,
we were prophets of motion,
priests and priestesses
of basslines and rhythm,
writing our prayers
with feet on sand,
with hands raised high
to the desert's stars.

Like Danielle,
we found our temple
in the pulse of sound,
our scripture
in the beat,
our prayers
in the pure joy
of kinetic devotion.

We didn't know
our last communion
would be that dawn,
our final blessing
the way music moved
through us like spirit,
before paradise
descended into hell.

Now when I dance,
I dance with ghosts—
my partners all
the ones who fell.
Each step a memory,
each beat a name,
each song a prayer
for those who danced
their last that day.

Barefoot Steps in Starlight

Sacred ground beneath
bare feet writing prayers in
the desert's cooling sand

Music becomes light
bodies transform into pure
spirit under stars

Three thousand hearts beat
as one beneath heaven's gaze—
flawless unity

Dawn approaches now
with its terrible message:
faith shall be tested

Some will never dance
again, some will dance always
with grief as partner

Music in the Ashes

We danced our prayers beneath the stars that
night,
Found God in motion, in the pure delight.

Each step a psalm, each gesture toward the
sky
A testament to life, to youth's birthright.

The music was our rabbi, priest, and guide,
Leading us toward dawn's approaching light.

Who knew our temple would become a grave?
Our prayers of joy transform to screams of
fright?

Some say God died that morning in the
sand—
Some say He wept, but could not stop the
blight.

Now when we dance, if dance we ever can,
We move with shadows, ghosts of lost delight.

Yet still we seek that sacred space again,
Where movement might restore what's lost to
night.

Heaven Turned Hell

We came to this heaven to dance,
To pray with our feet, take our chance
With joy pure and deep,

With rhythms to keep—
Then bullets shattered romance.

Our temple of music and light
Transformed in the dawn's early flight
To hell's waiting room,
Our dance floor a tomb,
Our prayers turned to screams in the night.

Yet some of us still dare to move,
Still seek out the rhythms that prove
Life flows in our veins,
Though marked now by pain—
Each dance a new prayer to improve.

When the Music Returns

Months later, at another festival,
I broke down crying—
the familiar pulse of bass,
the crowd's electric joy,
the raised hands silhouetted
against stage lights.

"Oh my God," I thought,
"I'm at a festival
and there are no missiles?
No rockets?
This is real?"

The tears came then,
joy and grief tangled
like dancers in the dark—
happiness to be alive,
to feel the music again,
mixed with memories
of those who'll never
dance another beat.

Now every festival
is both eulogy
and resurrection,
every dance move
both celebration
and remembrance.

We carry their rhythm
in our hearts,
their last dance

in our bones,
their prayers
in our motion.

Some find God in silence,
some in sacred halls—
we found divinity
in movement,
and lost it
in stillness,
and seek it still
in every beat
that dares us
to dance again.

The Missing

Some survivors faced a fate perhaps worse than death. Noa Argamani's abduction, seared into global memory, was captured on camera—her terrified face as she was torn from her boyfriend Avinatan and carried away on a motorcycle became one of the massacre's most haunting images. She endured 246 days of captivity, living "in fear every day, under extreme conditions" before her rescue. For many families, uncertainty became a special kind of torture. These poems capture both the agony of those taken hostage and the endless limbo of families waiting for news of

missing loved ones, hoping against hope that
silence doesn't mean the worst.

Carried Away

The video plays again and again:
Noa on the motorcycle,
reaching back toward Avinatan,
her face a mask of terror
we all now wear in our nightmares.

Two hundred forty-six days
she will count in darkness,
each sunrise a cruel parody,
each sunset a small death,
while he searches everywhere,
calls her name to empty air.

Their love story suspended
between that reaching hand
and its intended touch,
between that final glimpse
and the next they pray will come,
between the festival's joy
and Gaza's unrelenting darkness.

Some say the camera lies,
but this truth is etched in pixels:
the moment paradise fractured,
when music became screams,
when dance became flight,
when love became distance,
when morning became night.

Empty Chairs

We set their places at the table still,
These empty chairs that wait for their return.
Time passes, but our hope they can't yet kill.

Each morning brings fresh pain we must
distill
Into more waiting—how much more to learn?
We set their places at the table still.

No news is good news, so they say, until
The silence stretches longer, starts to burn.
Time passes, but our hope they can't yet kill.

Each phone call might bring word to cure or
kill,
Each knock the news for which we yearn.
We set their places at the table still.

Their rooms remain untouched upon the hill,
Their clothes still hang, their calendars still
turn.
Time passes, but our hope they can't yet kill.

This limbo is a special kind of ill,
A wound that gives no chance to heal or
burn.
We set their places at the table still.
Time passes, but our hope they can't yet kill.

Two Hundred Forty-Six Days

In Gaza's darkness, Noa counts the days in
breaths, in heartbeats, in moments between
terror. She lives in a world without sun,
without music, without the touch of those
who love her. Each day is an eternity of fear,
each night a century of dread. She holds
Avinatan's face in her memory like a talisman,

remembers the festival's lights, the freedom of
dance, the joy that seems now like a dream
from another life. Two hundred forty-six days
of choosing to survive, of breathing through
the fear, of keeping faith with those who
search for her. Two hundred forty-six days
before the light returns.

Calls for Repatriation

Families gather
holding photos high above—
faces frozen young
in moments before the storm
tore their futures all away

Signs demand return
of daughters, sons still missing—
some in Gaza's depths,
some in unmarked desert graves,
some in limbo's endless wait

Mothers cannot sleep
while children might still be found
breathing somewhere dark—

hope becomes a cruel friend
that will not let grief begin

Candles burn each night
in windows across the land—
lights to guide them home,
whether to warm embrace or
final resting place at last

Empty Rooms

Their beds stay made,
their phones still charged
in case they call,
their clothes still fresh
should they come home at all..

We dust their photos,
water their plants,
preserve their worlds
in perfect stasis,
waiting.

Some families know
their children rest

in sacred ground.
Some know their loved ones
suffer in Gaza's grip.

But we who don't know—
we live in parentheses,
in suspended time,
in the space between
was and is,
is and might be,
might be and never was.

We are the guardians
of empty rooms,
the keepers of
unanswered phones,
the watchers of
unwatched doors.

We live between
hope and grief,
unable to move forward,
afraid to look back,
frozen in the moment
when they were

here,
then gone.

Fathers' Rage

The fathers of Nova victims carry a unique burden—grief sharpened by fury, and love shaped by helplessness. Yoram Yehudai watched his son Ron's death unfold in real-time through text messages, the final one sent at 11:39 a.m.: "It'll be okay, love you." Eldad Adar, desperate to save his daughter Gili, raced toward the festival grounds as the massacre was ongoing, only to spend a week in agonizing uncertainty before learning of her death. Eyal Waldman used a phone tracking app to find where his daughter Danielle died, discovering evidence of a brutal ambush: "From the shells that we have

found, there were at least three guns that
were shooting at the car." These poems
capture both the immediate desperation of
fathers trying to save their children and the
aftermath of their devastating loss.

11:47 A.M.

The texts come steady until they cease:
11:39 – "It'll be okay, love you"
yellow heart emoji,
"we'll keep in touch."

Your son tries to protect you
even now,
even as the container
where he hides
fills with terror,
fills with others
seeking shelter.

At 11:47,
a lone gunman enters.
You learn this later,
watch the footage,

count the minutes
between his last message
and his last breath.

Eight minutes
between "love you"
and silence.
Eight minutes
between father and orphan.
Eight minutes
that will echo
through all your
unlived years.

Racing South

I drive toward gunfire, toward my child,
my father's heart a compass pointing south
to where my Gili needs me. Prayers run wild
through mind and spirit, terror chokes my
guts.

The festival grounds burn against the sky,
while all around, young people flee in fear.
I press the gas—my daughter must not die

alone, must know her father tried to near

her terror with his love. But roads are
blocked,
and chaos turns each route into a trap.
Time mocks me as my hopes are slowly
locked
in failure. Later, I will fill this gap

with rage at those who stopped me reaching
her,
whose barriers became her sepulcher.

Following the Signal

I track my daughter's final moments through
an app, following the blue dot that marked
her life to where it blinks out in the desert.
The car is there, riddled with bullets, each
hole a chapter in a story I don't want to read.
I count shell casings like a grim archaeologist:
three different guns, three different angles, no
chance of escape. They surrounded her, my
Danielle, my California girl who loved life
and music and was going to be married. The

evidence tells me everything: how they came
from multiple directions, how they sprayed
the car with automatic fire, how my child
died in a crossfire of hatred. I am a father
deciphering his daughter's last moments in
bullet holes and brass casings, in burnt metal
and broken glass. This is not how a father
should learn about his child's death—playing
forensic scientist in the desert where she
danced her last dance.

The Unkept Archive

No official came to tell us why,
No one sat to share our pain,
No one answered when we asked them, "Why
did all our children die in vain?"

The state that failed to guard their dance
Now fails to guard their memory.
We fathers rage at circumstance,
At doors that close on history.

We piece together on our own
The puzzle of their final hours,

While those who ought to make truth be
known
Hide silent in their distant towers.

Our children's blood cries from the sand,
Their stories beg to be revealed,
But silence creeps across the land,
And truth lies buried, unrepealed.

A Father's Voice

I will not seek revenge—
I've already lost the war,
says one father.
I want to know if my son's killer
fled to Gaza, was killed,
or sits in prison,
says another.
I have seen exactly how
she was murdered,
says a third,
as if precision might
dull the blade of loss.

We are the fathers
of October's children,
the ones who could not
save them,
the ones who read
their final texts,
track their final steps,
count the bullets
that took them,
document the details
that will not
bring them back.

We are the fathers
who must live
with knowing
or not knowing,
with arriving too late,
with helplessness
turned to stone,
with fury
that will never
find its mark.

We are the fathers
of the lost ones,
and our rage
is a quiet thing now,
a cold thing,
a patient thing
that will outlast
mountains.

A Generation Lost

The Nova massacre devastated an entire community. Three hundred and sixty-four lives were stolen in the span of a single morning—young people who represented Israel's vibrant future. For survivors like Danielle Gelbaum, every return to a festival brings memories: "There is not even one time that I don't have memories of my friends who were murdered." Ofri Rahum lost multiple family members at once: her pregnant sister, her sister's fiancé, and her uncle. These poems capture the collective trauma of a community that lost not just individuals, but entire social circles, future families, and a generation's worth of dreams.

For the 364

Three hundred sixty-four hearts stopped that
day—
each one a universe of hopes and dreams,
each one a child some parent raised with care,
each one a future that will never be.

Three hundred sixty-four last morning
breaths,
exhaled as music turned to screams and fire.
Three hundred sixty-four stories cut short,
three hundred sixty-four flames extinguished.

Some were medics, rushing toward the hurt,
some were dancers lost in morning prayer,
some were lovers planning future days,
some were siblings sharing one last laugh.

A generation's light snuffed out at dawn,
their absence now an echo that lives on.

Re'im's Fields

The festival grounds lie empty now,
but memory fills the space
with ghosts of what was lost:

Here, a medical student
danced her last dance
before the bullets found her.

There, a young couple
shared their final kiss
before the world ended.

In that corner, friends
took their last selfie,
forever young and smiling.

By that tree, a brother
called his sister's name
one final time.

The desert holds
these moments now,
pressed like flowers

between pages of time:

Three thousand gathered,
three hundred sixty-four fell,
thousands more carry scars
visible and invisible.

This field has become
both graveyard and memorial,
where every grain of sand
remembers someone's child.

A Village of Mourning

In every neighborhood, someone knows
someone who was there. Six degrees of
separation have collapsed to one or none—we
are all tethered to this loss. The local coffee
shop misses its regular barista. The university
holds empty seats in lecture halls. The dance
studio's mirror reflects absences. A whole
generation has been carved into those who
died, those who survived, and those who carry
both the dead and the living in their hearts.

autumn leaves falling—
each one bears the name of those
we lost that morning

empty chairs waiting
in cafes across the land—
youth cut down in bloom

We Are the Desert's Cry

We are the desert's cry of pain,
Three hundred voices called in vain,
A generation's light gone dark,
Each death a wound, a burning mark
Upon our collective domain.

Young dreams now scattered like the rain
That never falls on this terrain—
We are the desert's cry of pain,
Three hundred voices called in vain.

No future will be quite the same,
No joy unmarked by loss and shame.

Each empty chair, each silent phone
Reminds us we are not alone—
We are the desert's cry of pain.

Empty Tents

The festival grounds hold only ghosts,
Where thousands danced at break of day.
A generation's dreams lie close
The festival grounds hold only ghosts.
Three hundred sixty-four we lost,
Their music silenced, turned to clay.
The festival grounds hold only ghosts,
Where thousands danced at break of day.

The morning wind still carries notes
Of songs that died in October's haze.
Each empty tent becomes a host
To memories of better days.
The festival grounds hold only ghosts,
Where thousands danced at break of day.

The Weight of Living

For those who survived, living itself became a burden laced with complexity. Vlada Patapov, the "Lady in Red" whose escape photo became iconic, expressed unshakeable survivor's guilt: "If I had one wish, it would be to have told everyone at the festival one hour before the attack that something was going to happen so everyone could have got away." Jenny Sividia chose a different path, alchemizing her survival into purpose, spending time at a Healing Place for Nova survivors, saying "The trauma turns into organic waste that supports something's growth." These poems explore both the guilt of surviving and the

responsibility survivors feel to honor those
who didn't make it out.

Why Me?

A single step this way, not that—
The difference between breath and death.
Why was I spared? I wonder at
The randomness of who has left.

The difference between breath and death
Could be a car that wouldn't start,
The randomness of who departed,
The choices that would tear apart

Could be a car that wouldn't start,
A premonition, sudden fear,
The choices that would tear apart
The futures that were drawing near.

A premonition, sudden fear—
Why was I spared? I wonder at
The futures that were drawing near,
A single step this way, not that.

Step by Step

Like Raz, I found myself
tying tourniquets
instead of taking chemo,
trying to save others
and failing.

The universe has
its own strange arithmetic:
subtract the cancer
that should have killed me,
add the bullets
that killed my friends instead.

I survived that morning,
survived six months
of mother feeding me,
survived the guilt
of being here at all.

Each breath I take
belongs to someone else,
each step I walk
leaves footprints

on borrowed time.

What do you do
with a life that's yours
only because others
lost theirs?
You live it twice as hard,
twice as full,
twice as meaningful—
once for yourself,
once for them.

The Lady in Red

The camera caught me fleeing in my dress,
A splash of red against the desert sand.
They thought me dead or taken—I confess
Sometimes I wish I were, to understand

Why I was saved while others had to fall,
Why I came home to hold my daughter tight
While other mothers pace an empty hall,
Their children lost to that October night.

If I could turn time back, I'd sound the alarm,
I'd warn them all an hour before the storm,
I'd save each dancer from approaching harm—
But memory holds me in its rigid form:

A woman running in a crimson dress,
Survival marked by such randomness.

Organic Growth

Trauma plants its seeds
deep in survival's garden—
what might bloom from pain?

Memory becomes
compost for tomorrow's growth—
grief feeds healing's roots

We who lived must tend
these gardens of remembrance,
must water the soil
with our tears,
must plant new life
in ground that drank
our friends' blood,

must believe that beauty
can grow from horror,
that purpose can sprout
from pain's dark earth.

A Vow of Living

I carry your names
like prayer beads,
clicking them off
in my midnight thoughts:

This breath for Maya,
this step for David,
this laugh for Sarah,
this tear for Ron.

I live because you died,
or you died because I lived—
the math of survival
never quite adds up.

But I promise you this:
I will live fully enough
for both of us,

will dance twice as hard,
love twice as deep,
fight twice as long,
dream twice as big.

I will make my survival
mean something,
will turn this guilt
into purpose,
this pain into power,
this grief into growth.

I will live
because you cannot,
will tell your stories
because you cannot,
will carry your light
because you cannot,
will dance your dances
because you cannot.

This is my vow
to you who fell
so I could rise:
Your death

will not be
the end of your story.
I am your witness,
your voice,
your legacy,
your living memorial.

The World Watches

The Nova massacre shocked the global conscience. Survivors like Yuval Raphael spoke before the UN Human Rights Council, ensuring the world could not look away. Natalie Sanandaji, an American caught in the massacre, dedicated herself to fighting antisemitism and ensuring the victims are not forgotten: "I can no longer simply enjoy the life I once had... I will never be the same person after what I saw and felt on Oct. 7." These poems capture both the international outcry and the struggle to make the world understand the true horror of what happened that morning.

We Testify

Before the nations gathered,
we stand and speak
the unspeakable:

How young women begged
before bullets found them,
how killers laughed
while ending lives,
how music turned to screams
in desert dawn.

We bring our wounds
to marble halls,
our nightmares
to microphones,
our dead
to the world's conscience.

Some turn away,
some deny,
some try to twist
our truth to lies.

But we who lived
must speak for those
who cannot speak,
must show our scars
to those who doubt,
must make the world
remember.

This is our testimony:
We were there.
We saw.
We lived.
We remember.
We demand justice.

News Flashes Worldwide

Headlines break like dawn—
massacre at music fest—
world stops, holds its breath

Footage plays worldwide:
girl torn from boyfriend, terror
caught in camera's eye

Faces of the lost
stare from every screen and page—
youth cut down in bloom

Global conscience stirs—
some turn away from the truth,
some cannot forget

Hashtags and Heartbreak

The world scrolls through scenes of our pain,
As headlines flash grief once again.
　　Some share what they see,
　　Some let our truth be,
While others deny what is plain.

#BringThemHome trends day by day,
As hostages' families pray.
　　Each photo shared
　　Shows someone who cared,
Whose future was stolen away.

The truth spreads in pixels and posts,
As witnesses share what we lost.

Each story told
Helps truth unfold,
Though some would deny at all costs.

An Ode to the Photographs

These images that broke the world's heart:
A girl on a motorcycle, reaching back,
A woman in red, running for her life,
Young bodies scattered on festival grounds,
Parents holding photos of the missing,
Empty chairs waiting for the taken.

Each pixel tells a story that must live,
Each frame captures what we can't forget,
Each shot ensures the world must see
What happened in that desert dawn
When music died and terror reigned
And youth was stolen from the sand.

Let these pictures pierce denial's veil,
Let them stand as witness through the years,
Let them remind those who would forget
That here three hundred sixty-four
Young lives were ended in their prime,

That here humanity was tested,
And here their story must be told.

Never Again, Again

The world once vowed this would not be,
That mass graves would not fill again,
That such horror we would not see.

But promises break easily
When hatred rises, fierce and plain.
The world once vowed this would not be.

Three hundred sixty-four set free
To dance, then slaughtered in death's reign,
That such horror we would not see.

Their stories spread across the sea,
Some hearts are moved, some souls remain
Unmoved—though we vowed this would not
be.

We who survived must guarantee
Their memory does not wane in vain,
That such horror we would not see.

So speak we must, so must we be
The voice that echoes this refrain:
The world once vowed this would not be,
That such horror we would not see.

Art From Ashes

From the depths of trauma, survivors found healing through creative expression. Yuval Raphael, who survived eight hours under bodies in a bomb shelter, found salvation in songs: "Music is one of the strongest ingredients in my healing process." She went from having no singing experience to winning Israel's Rising Star and representing her country at Eurovision. Jenny Sividia, who lost her brother Shlomi, found purpose at a Healing Place for survivors, saying "The trauma turns into organic waste that supports something's growth." These poems explore how art, music, and community become lifelines for those learning to live with their memories.

A Healing Place

We gather in circles, survivors and bereaved, our pain like clay in our hands. Some mold it into sculptures, some paint it onto canvas, some sing it into the air. Here, trauma becomes raw material for creation. A mother who lost her son throws pots on a wheel, each vessel a container for her grief. A young man who hid for hours under bodies now plays guitar, his fingers finding the notes his voice cannot yet speak. A woman who lost her sister weaves tapestries in red and gold, threading memory into meaning. We are all artists here, though we never meant to be. Our medium is loss, our palette is pain, but somehow beauty emerges from these broken pieces of ourselves. "The trauma turns into organic waste," Jenny tells us, and we understand: even the darkest soil can feed new growth.

Canvas of Tears

Each brushstroke holds a memory of pain,
Each color mixed with tears we cannot cry.
The canvas bears the weight of all we've seen,
The horror rendered just to exorcise.

Here, crimson bleeds like dawn on desert
sand,
There, darkness pools in corners of our fear.
The shapes of loss take form beneath our
hands,
As art transforms the grief we cannot bear.

Some paint the faces of the ones they lost,
Some abstract nightmares into healing forms,
Some trace the line between the saved and
cost,
Some find peace in colors bright and warm.

Through art, we speak what words cannot
contain:
The truth of loss, the hope that still remains.

Hands Holding Clay

Fingers press the clay
shaping formless grief into
something we can hold—
each vessel we create here
carries memories of them

In the potter's wheel
trauma spins and transforms shape
under gentle hands—
what was shapeless pain becomes
beauty we can understand

From the kiln emerge
vessels fired by our grief
stronger than before—
like us, they have passed through flame
and survived transformation

RESILIENCE

Remember them in every stroke of art
Emerging from the darkness of that day,
Seeking light in colors, forms, and clay,

Insisting beauty rise from pain's deep heart.
Letting trauma feed creative soil,
Inviting healing through each thing we make,
Ensuring that their memory will take
New forms that time and death cannot
despoil.
Crafting hope from horror's raw material,
Expressing what mere words cannot convey.

Together We Rise

In art therapy rooms,
we paint our nightmares
into submission.

In music circles,
we sing our grief
into harmony.

In dance studios,
we move our trauma
through our bodies
until it transforms
into grace.

In writing workshops,
we give voice
to the unspeakable,
turn our screams
into poetry.

In pottery classes,
we reshape our pain
into vessels
that can hold
both grief and hope.

Yuval found her voice
beneath the bodies,
carried it out
into the light,
let it soar
for all the angels
who fell that day.

Jenny weaves her brother's
memory into tapestries
of healing,
lets his absence
feed new growth.

We create
because we must,
because art
can hold
what hearts cannot,
because beauty
can emerge
from horror,
because making
is a form
of surviving,
of thriving,
of testifying.

Together,
we transform
our darkness
into light,
our trauma
into truth,
our pain
into purpose.

This too
is resistance:
to create
in the face
of destruction,
to make art
from ashes,
to find beauty
even here.

The Music Returns

For some survivors, returning to music became both restorative and excruciating. Yuval Raphael, who survived eight hours under bodies in a shelter, found unexpected solace in singing: "Music is one of the strongest ingredients in my healing process." She went from having no prior singing experience to winning Israel's Rising Star and representing her country at Eurovision. Danielle Gelbaum's first return to a festival brought overwhelming emotion: "I thought to myself: 'Oh my God, I am at a festival... and I'm not seeing any missiles? No rockets? ... This is real.' And I started crying my eyes out."

These poems explore the complex journey of
reclaiming music and dance after the
massacre.

Under the Spotlight, Again

From the shelter's darkness,
from beneath the bodies,
from eight hours of holding death
at bay with stillness,
Yuval rises to sing.

No one who watched her
on Rising Star's stage
could see the weight she carried:
shrapnel still lodged
in head and leg,
memories still lodged
deeper still.

But when she opens her mouth,
when she lets her voice soar
through "Dancing Queen,"
she sings for all the angels
who danced their last

that morning,
transforms trauma
into tribute.

From Eurovision's stage
she will tell their story
in the universal language
of song,
will show the world
that music outlasts
massacre,
that harmony defeats
horror,
that the voice that survived
beneath the dead
now rises
to touch the stars.

Surviving Song

She steps onto the dance floor, trembling
now,
The bass beats like her heart once beat in fear.
The memories flood back, but still somehow
She forces herself to be present here.

The lights flash like the rockets used to do,
The crowd's roar echoes gunfire in her mind,
But slowly, as the music pulses through,
She feels the rhythm leave the past behind.

Each movement is a victory tonight,
Each beat reclaimed from terror's heavy toll.
The ghosts of friends dance with her in the
light,
Their memory making broken pieces whole.

This is her revolution: choosing joy,
Though grief still echoes in the melody,
Finding the strength to dance, create, employ
The music as a path toward being free.

The DJ's Turntable

The music plays, though changed by what we
know—
Each beat recalls that morning's deadly rain,
Yet still we choose to let the rhythm flow.

Like Daniel, saved that day not long ago,
Who spins his records through his healing
pain,
The music plays, though changed by what we
know.

Some frequencies bring memories of woe,
Some songs now carry weights they can't
contain,
Yet still we choose to let the rhythm flow.

Each festival becomes both yes and no—
Both tribute to the dead and life's refrain.
The music plays, though changed by what we
know.

We dance between the present and the glow
Of memories we'll never see again,
Yet still we choose to let the rhythm flow.

This is our way to heal, to learn, to grow:
Through darkness, still we sing this sweet
refrain.
The music plays, though changed by what we
know,

Yet still we choose to let the rhythm flow.

Melody in Minor Key

First notes hesitate—
like birds testing broken wings,
learning flight again

Music carries grief
but also carries us home—
healing in each note

Eurovision Dream

When Yuval takes the stage in Basel,
she will carry with her
forty voices silenced,
eleven who survived,
eight hours under bodies,
one grenade that changed
everything.

She will sing
not just for Israel,
but for every young soul

who danced at Nova,
for every dream
cut short at dawn,
for every note
that terror tried
to silence.

Her voice will rise
from the ashes
of that morning,
will soar beyond
the boundaries
of nations,
will prove that music
cannot be killed
by bullets,
that art outlives
atrocity,
that even from
the darkest shelter,
a song can rise
to touch the world.

This is her victory:
not just surviving,

but singing,
not just remembering,
but creating,
not just witnessing,
but transmuting
trauma into triumph,
pain into performance,
grief into glory.

From the shelter
to the spotlight,
from death's shadow
to center stage—
her journey tells us
that even after
the darkest night,
music finds its way
back into the world.

One Year Later

At the one-year memorial, survivors and families gathered to remember. Ofri Rahum expressed the surreal nature of time: "Time flies. I don't believe it's been a year. It's like a dream I want to wake up from." For some, like Eldad Adar, father of Gili, the pain was compounded by official silence: "No official has come to properly explain to us, to sit with us, to ask us anything." These poems capture both the weight of remembrance and the ongoing struggle for truth, as survivors and families work to ensure the Nova massacre is never forgotten or denied.

One Year Anniversary

We gather in Tel Aviv,
holding candles against
the darkness that lingers
even in daylight.

Three hundred sixty-four flames
flicker in the evening breeze—
one for each life lost,
one for each story
cut brutally short.

Ofri stands among us,
still waiting for her sister
to return from a trip
that never ends,
time frozen like a photograph
from before the world changed.

Parents clutch photos
of children forever young,
forever dancing
in that last dawn.

Eldad demands answers
from officials who never came,
from a government
that failed twice:
first to protect,
then to remember.

We light our candles,
speak their names,
tell their stories,
guard their memory
against time's erosion,
against denial's shadow,
against forgetting's mercy.

Gathering the Stories

We piece together what was lost that day,
Each witness adding threads of memory,
Each survivor's voice helping to say
What future generations must still see.

Here Rada tells of women begging life,
There Yuval speaks of hours beneath the dead,
While Noa's tale of captive months of strife

Reminds us some wounds have not yet bled.

We document each detail, large and small,
Each text message, each final phone call
home,
Each act of courage, each heroic fall,
Each story carved in memory's living stone.

Truth must survive when we are dust and air,
These stories must outlive our time of grief,
These testimonies must remain to bear
Witness long past our own lives' brief relief.

Bearing Witness

One year has passed, yet time stands strangely
still,
As memory keeps its grip on Re'im's hill.

We gather now to speak their names once
more,
To count the cost upon that desert floor.

Three hundred sixty-four young lives erased,
Their futures stolen, dreams forever chased.

We who survived must bear this witness true,
Must tell their stories, old yet always new.

Must fight against forgetting's gentle balm,
Must keep our memories sharp, our voices
calm.

Must document each detail, fact, and name,
Must hold accountable those most to blame.

For history turns too quickly from such pain,
Unless we make their memory remain.

Monuments of Dust

The state that failed to guard them
fails again to hear their stories,
fails again to seek the truth,
fails again to honor memory.

We document ourselves:
fathers tracking bullet casings,
mothers recording testimonies,
siblings preserving photos,
survivors writing memoirs.

We build our own monuments:
in poetry, in song,
in art, in dance,
in every act of memory
that refuses to let go,
that demands to be heard,
that insists on truth.

We are the keepers
of this sacred history,
the guardians
of their stories,
the witnesses
who will not
be silenced.

Candles at Dusk

We gather as the sun sets, just as they
gathered that morning for what would be
their final dawn. Each of us holds a candle,
each flame a life, each light a memory we
refuse to let die. The names are read—three
hundred sixty-four times the air vibrates with
loss. Parents who lost children, children who
lost parents, siblings who lost siblings, friends
who lost friends. We are bound together in
this circle of remembrance, this community
of the bereaved and the surviving. Some find
comfort in the sharing of grief, some find
purpose in the demand for truth, some find
strength in the simple act of standing
together. As darkness falls, our candles form a
constellation of memory, a galaxy of grief, a
universe of love that refuses to be
extinguished.

   evening descends now—
   three hundred sixty-four lights
   pierce October's dark

each flame holds a name
each name holds a universe
of love and of loss

together we stand
guarding memory's candles
against time's dark wind

Reclaiming The Desert

The desert that witnessed such horror must somehow be reclaimed. Rada Rashed speaks of having "two birth dates" now—his original one and October 7, when he was "reborn" after surviving. Daniel Vaknin, the DJ rescued by a Holocaust survivor, insists we must "choose light... no matter how much darkness you've seen." These final seven poems (completing our collection of 107) explore how a place of tragedy might be transformed into sacred ground, how memory and hope might coexist, and how the desert might once again hear music instead of screams.

Return to Sand

Desert, you who drank their blood,
you who heard their final prayers,
you who held their dancing feet
before you held their fallen forms—
we return to you now.

Not to forget,
but to remember.
Not to erase,
but to inscribe
their names in your sand,
their stories in your stones,
their dreams in your dawn.

We come to plant gardens
in soil that tasted tears,
to sing new songs
where silence fell,
to dance again
where they danced last.

You are witness, desert—
to both their joy

and their ending,
to both their freedom
and their fall,
to both what was
and what might be.

Hold their memory
in your endless sands,
but let new life
take root here too.

On This Day, We Remember

On this sacred ground we stand and say:
Remember them, but choose to live.
Their dance lives on another way.
On this sacred ground we stand and say
Their memory lights our forward way,
Their joy is what we now must give.
On this sacred ground we stand and say:
Remember them, but choose to live.

Across the Gaza Border

The desert stretches endless, knows no line
That humans draw to separate their pain.
The wind that carries music, carries rain
Across these borders we call yours and mine.

Three hundred sixty-four we lost that day,
Their futures scattered in October's sand.
Yet hope, like morning light across the land,
Must somehow find its resurrection way.

For peace must come, though now it seems so
far,
And music must return to heal these scars,
And dance must rise again beneath the stars,
Though changed forever by the things we are.

The desert holds both memory and dreams—
Both what was lost and what redemption
means.

Two Birthdays

Rada counts two births:
one in spring, one in fall's fire—
life renewed through death

Desert witnessed both:
first breath and rebirth through flames,
sand remembering

Now we plant new seeds
where blood watered barren ground—
life from death must grow

Morning breaks again
over Re'im's haunted fields—
hope still dares to bloom

A Second Sunrise

The sun still rises over Re'im's fields, just as it
did that morning. But now its light falls
differently across the sand, touching places
that have become sacred through suffering,
holy through horror. We return with seeds to

plant, with songs to sing, with dances to dance—changed, but still living. The desert remembers everything: the music of that night, the terror of that dawn, the silence that followed. But the desert also knows renewal, knows how life pushes through even the driest sand, knows how morning always follows night. We come back changed, carrying our dead within us, but also carrying their dreams, their joy, their love of life. This is how we honor them: by refusing to let this place remain only a grave, by insisting it also be a garden.

Souls in the Wind

They dance now forever in desert wind,
Their spirits free in the desert wind.

Each grain of sand holds memory's trace,
Each story soars in the desert wind.

Three hundred sixty-four names we speak
As prayer dies in the desert wind.

Yet here new life must somehow bloom,
Hope never dies in the desert wind.

We plant their dreams in sacred sand,
While love flies in the desert wind.

107 Beats of the Heart

One hundred and seven poems
for October 7—
one beat of the heart
for each moment that changed us,
one pulse of memory
for each life that touched us,
one breath of witness
for each story that shapes us.

We end where we began:
in the desert,
under stars,
with music.

But now we know
what the sand remembers,
what the wind carries,
what the dawn witnessed.

We are changed,
but still dancing.
We are wounded,
but still singing.
We are grieving,
but still living.

Let the desert hold
both our joy and our sorrow,
both our dancing and our dying,
both our music and our mourning.

Let this place be
both memorial and miracle,
both graveyard and garden,
both ending and beginning.

Let us be
both witnesses and warriors,
both mourners and makers,
both memory and hope.

This is how we go on:
carrying their light,
playing their music,
dancing their dreams,
telling their stories,
planting their future
in desert sand
that remembers
everything.